CAN'T FORGET
THE MOTOR CITY...

NEW POEMS BY
JOSEPH NICKS

Can't Forget The Motor City...

First Edition Copyright © 2018

ISBN 978-0-9971257-2-6

Published by Blue Jay Ink
Ojai, California
bluejayink.com

Book Design by Blue Jay Ink
Cover art by Ojai Digital
Photography by Nathan Dumlao and Pedro Lastra
via unsplash.com.

Back cover and interior:
Detroit Industry, North Wall, 19... Rivera, Diego
(1886-1957) Credit: Detroit Institute of Arts, USA
Gift of Edsel B. Ford/Bridgeman Images

This is MagPie Book #18.
Visit JosephNicks.com for a complete list of
Magnesium Pie publications.

One-fourth of the proceeds from the sale of these
books is contributed to a fund that benefits the
following organizations:

The American Cetacean Society
Bat Conservation International
Black Mamba Anti-Poaching Unit
International Bird Rescue
The International Union for Conservation of Nature
Panthera.org

For Pirate –
my last dog,
who would've
been 50 this year

For Prince –
my first dog,
who would've
been 60 this year

For my sister Carla,
who still lives and works
on the third coast, at the
hub of the Great Lakes

Can't Forget The Motor City...

★previously published (see Appendix A)

One hundred years ago...

1918: He was born in Detroit, the son of Italian immigrants. Died there too, 93 years later. From what I can gather, he worked just about every day of every year except maybe those first five – and those last two. Once they took his driver's license, he was pretty much done for.

He and his kin were people of collar – blue collar. No bullshit mafioso Al Pacino/Robert De Niro-types here. No embarrassingly silly-assed bada bing – bada boom John Travolta/Andrew Dice Clay circus clowns either. Just urban-steeled people who knew how to shut up and work. Their toughness lay more in what they could take than what they could dish out. Of course, if you had a mind to fuck with any one of them, it was definitely at your own risk.

1925: Her family came in off the prairies of North Dakota, farm-hardened Scandinavian folk without much time for fooling around – or much patience for those who did. Seemed like they were busy every waking hour.

But there was still something profoundly wrong with these people; the subservience they expected of their women. She would suffer for that all of her years.

1956: Somehow, these two lineages became entangled. My earliest recollections are of the back-then green and quiet side streets of Eight Mile and Livernois on the city's west side. Razed to a vacant corner grasslot now, the house at 20254 San Juan Drive gave me a second-story window to the world – and the embryonic stirrings that have both plagued me and inspired me all my life.

the 1960s: It was during my six-and-a-half-year residency here that I first became aware of differences. Primarily of the extra-hominid diversity out there that would fuel my lifelong biological studies – all these amazing other organisms so different from us yet so needful of the same things: air, water, food, space, and others of their kind.

Then there were the more subtle infra-species nuances that should've been a cause for celebration but somehow became the fodder for the inequity that has long been an arbitrarily-imposed facet of the human condition.

We were white kids. We were black kids. We were an infinite array of hues and tinctures in between. And we never thought to make anything of that other than how it enhanced our individuality – until some outside forces taught a surprisingly large number of us to do so. Still, it was a lesson some of us never learned – and swear we never will.

the 1970s: The spirit of the '60s did its best to persevere. But John left Paul and Paul left Art and Motown left Motown for the greener (hyper-irrigated) pastures of Hollywood. Though some of the best of the '60s spilled over into the early '70s, by mid-decade, the whole civilized world seemed firmly in the grip of either glitter-ball shake-your-booty disco dementia or else the head-banging stupefaction of heavily-metaled necrophiles. Don't even get me started on what happened to our cars.

Come 1974, I was off to the Wayne Assembly Plant and Henry Ford Community College simultaneously in a tug-of-war I pulled on from both sides for half a decade.

The factories laid us off, called us back, laid us off again and in between we studied – and worked whatever two-dollar-an-hour jobs we could get so we could buy gas, food, and books.

By 1978, I'd taken every class at HFCC that was of any use to a biology major. There was no way I'd be able to afford to attend any of the four-year universities – not on minimum wages.

My car was being eaten away by the road salt of winter and my dog was battling heartworm for the second time.

the 1980s: I finally saw that I had little choice but to pack up my books and my bones and my vinyl and my dog and point my '68 Cyclone southwest to Cal State Long Beach at the end of the summer of 1979. Got a job with the Sanitation Districts of L.A. County at the pollution control plant in Carson, balancing work and school for the next decade or so. Sort of a lukewarm happy ending.

Of course it didn't end there, as anyone who's ever been torn between two homes can tell you. I never got over that migration. Not a week goes by that I don't second-guess myself and wonder what might've been.

I still go back, maybe once a year, to check in on my sister and what's left of the rest of my family and old friends. I always figured it was just them I was going back for.

But as soon as I get back there, I go walking.
I go remembering. I go feeling everything I felt
when I was just another anonymous blue-collar kid
with a head full of half-assed ideas and a heart full
of pounding, resounding things I couldn't wrap my
hands around. And I get to thinking. About how
lucky I was to get out. About how luck had nothing
to do with it as my back and other joints are quick to
remind me. About how it's high time I got back.
About how Southeastern Michigan and I still seem
to have some unfinished business to attend to –
though I can't quite figure out just exactly what it is.

And though there's not a sound around, I'm
somehow haunted by that song that belonged
to Jimmy Ruffin...

This Place

I have lived this simmering sameness
throughout many a change of place

these same books have come to rest
on many different shelves,
this same music's swirled aloft
through many different rooms,
these same pictures have been posted
up on many different walls
and these same eyes have gazed
through many different windows

this place has torn me
from my sleep each dawn
and plunged me deep again
into the dreamless afterhours

this place has welcomed me
and worn on me
and left its mark in me

I have cursed this place,
endured this place
and immersed myself in this place,
holed up in this place for the winter
and fled this place in the spring

and every day I pen another page –
the only way to make it "home"
until I somehow make it home,
the gist of which has
eluded me since 1979
in every shoulder
I've looked over
since that time

Breverence

in a diner in the desert
on my way to where knows when,
the air feels painfully familiar
though I'm quite certain
I have never breathed
a breath like this before

seems as though it's been
the better part of forever
I have heaved against this earth
and my own mortality,
yearning mid-eternity
for just a little larger look
than the spark here in the darkness
of the eons gone unlit
and the ages
we assume are yet to come

another nanoscopic wake
in the ripples of infinity,
I know that I'll be dead

far longer than I ever was
alive

Eternitude

listen to how silently
these first stray beams
of freshly-broken dawn
have pierced the soft steel-grey
of the brooding harbor sky

watch again how gleamingly
they're cast across
the silver thalassic plateau
highlighting ship-peppered forever
lending shimmer to the sea

breathe deeply of how many times
some one or another among us
has paused to quench
both thirsty eye
and hungry heart at once

remember how unforgettable
each freeze-frame forged in flesh
and blood and bone once was —
as instantaneous awareness
disappears into the littleness of now

Just This Minute *(my 31,423,184th)*

I fell in love on Signal Hill,
downtown on Pine Avenue,
up on the bluffs of Ocean Blvd,
the after-depths of Colorado Lagoon

from Queen Mary to The Circle,
Oil Islands to LBX,
the ninth floor of The McIntosh
to The Gerald Desmond Bridge –
there was a lot to fall in love with
way back when

now, I'm no older
than the youngest of these places –
I'm still as walking as I was
and they're still there in all their
changedness of face

though recently, these steps
aren't so spring-loaded –
I find I keep preparing for the fall

but for now's another summer
come to call:
another hundred fifty days
to work out in the sun;
another hundred fifty nights
to get some writing done

because one of these old years,
everything's still gonna be here
except for me

Slopeshot #99

up on the hill again today –
I went up there to take
another picture with my pen

it's smaller than the last time
which in turn was smaller
than the time before

that is, the hill itself's
the same size –
its viridescence is the only
thing that shrinks
until the tiniest of peaks
is all we working folk can get

the green of yester-vistas
that lent lung to
wounded spirit,
harried thoughtfulness,
and ache of day alike
has given way to
a different kind of green –
one man's reality
is another's realty

On Sadder Day Mournings

Mojave Desert musings #66

in the read-eyed wake
of faded flimsy promise
piling up on top of sadder days
too seasoned to be fooled
and yet still shoring up the weak
end of a quarter of a month

the cycling of the sun and
more importantly the moon,
the creeping planetation
of both mars and mercury,
cosmic jupiter-and-saturn's
far-away gigantitude –
all have lent their
pondered presence
to perturbing my inertia

and venus in the evening
helps me come into my own
to tap the world's nocturning
and drink deeply of the darkness
while it dominates the dome

but venus in the mourning
of another night's demise
can only bring me to my senses,
once again to realize

that if the dawn weren't prone to breaking
with such stubborn repetition,
there'd really be no need for evening –
there'd be nothing for the twilight to repair

The Wind And Longing Road

there she blows –
I've known her well,
unseen but not unfelt
abreast of every highway
I have travelled in its time
to the tune of troubled traffic
en route to reckoning

but, come the midnight drone
of the once-again alone,
who've lost enough to have found
those dark elusive passages
that nurture every thinking,
every feeling

who roll with every crossward gust,
who pitch with topographic rise and fall,
who yaw in detour and deflection
yet somehow motor on

who persevere in the descent of a divided continent
giving way to the thunderstorming plain
and the interplay of songscape and terrain

these stubborn few persist
despite the flickering of faith
now only twilit by the same
sun-ups-and-downs
they chase the quick
horizon back around,
gone hungrily half-hopeful
in the wind and longing road

Six Feet

I'm sure I'm not the first
to find a mere six feet of soil
to be of such unfathomable depth

but thirty-three years later
I still can't unremember
those fifteen

those near-sleepless sixty seasons
from summer '68 until the fall of '83
when all distance seemed to shrink
before our unrelenting run
through disillusioned days
and newfound nights alike

whatever hours we could steal
from the wicked lords of labor
and the slavery of study
we devoted to the fleetfulness of foot

and so we ran

for our lives
and what we thought
they'd someday be...

somehow it slipped my notice
that our life-clocks spun
at different rates

and up on Signal Hill
in the shovel–chuff of dirt
before the dawn
I committed him to memory
and I turned into the grey

to walk
no more to run
the long remaining years alone

where we once were six feet strong
now I find I'm four foot short

Until You Walk

you go four-legged on the floor
across the room to get somewhere
of no intention, consequence
or recollection – a pudgy little
vague-abond asprawl of all the world
with no direction

next day an upright tetrapod
forsaking half his limbs
and thumbing unopposably onward,
gone viral on the rest of the biosphere

you can crawl and you can toddle
but, until you (learn to) walk,
you'll never understand

you venture forth upon
unclaimed terrain
until you think you've found a place
to plant your flag
and then proceed to carve up parcels
of now-eyeless reality

next day your deeds outnumber you
by many hundredfold –
your fellows will pay dearly
to stake out their rightful plots;
signed, sealed, delivered, unrecycled

you can drive, you can be driven
but, until you (opt to sometimes) walk,
you'll never understand

you rise above all hopes and dreams
of those teeming underlings
some thousand miles closer to the land –
the more you make them want,
the harder they will work

next day you circle Earth, besmirked
at just how small it all has grown,
product now exceeding all resource
in soon-to-be-effluent affluence

you can fly, you can go wireless
but, until you (remember how to) walk,
you'll never understand

I survey sky-scraped expanses,
no acre of which I would choose
to lay any claim to

next day I'm up and on my way
to where we may yet build
a better future (by not building) –
the world is still a pretty big place
when you walk out into it

you can surf entangled in the net,
you can virtually zoom
from continents and seas
to streets and addresses
but, until you walk again,
you'll never understand

What Is Left To Do

when, despite the tortured writhing
of your conscience
and the tearing of your thoughts
against your feelings –

despite your own life-weariness,
forebodings teeming faster
than regrets

you find you're simply
not creative enough
to have that nervous breakdown?

your heart's too
god-damned stubborn
to forgo its further beatings?

there's nothing you care
enough about
to warrant an addiction to?

well, I guess you simply wake
to rub the sleep out of your eyes,
curse another working day,
and climb back up on top
of stiff and creaking joints
to haul your sorry skeleton
back out into the naked light
of no alternative

Nobody IX

me, I'm Nobody IX,
a person of no particular color –
tinted by the wind,
the rain, and the blinding
white light of mid-day

yes, I'm Nobody IX,
an individual of as yet
no discernible distinction –
as invisible as air
and all the space you stare
so blankly through

see, I'm Nobody IX,
and I come from a long, long line
of Nobodies gone nowhere
but about their back-bent business –
tilling up their daily bread
and on and on anonymous
to further someone else's cause,
conceit and appetite

hell, I'm just Nobody IX,
the last of a long-dead breed –
the one mistake in all my ancestry
was their fecundity,
this perpetuated peasantry
that stokes the dynamo
with teeming generations
of dead wood and meat on the hoof

oh no, I am Nobody IX –
there's not gonna be a Nobody X

Daydread *(tomorrophobia)*

I hope tomorrow's just a day
and not a minute more than that –
it takes so long

to try to do what you were doing
and what everybody else
wants you to do

I hope tomorrow's just a day
and not the reckoning I know
I'll face somewhen

for every promise I have failed
to deliver – for being everyone
but who I've tried to be

I hope tomorrow's just a day
and not so much of what I've feared
it would become

another new today
unequipped to do much more
than rage against a brave new world
that gorges on the future
and hemorrhages yesterly
to stain posterity

Contemperature

within the heated traffic
of the stifling afternoon,
the future's getting smaller
by the day

though I pledge no allegiance
to the present that we give,
this time we trade away
to earn our keep

no I know just where the sun sets
before it sets anywhere else
and I'll be there to catch that
wherever still life breathes –
out where the night moves
only in its fourth dimension

because I've learned a thing or two
about the Earth, this age old orb
that contradicts itself at every turn
as west spins into east spins into west
and early becomes late enough
to somehow become early again

and back among the masses
where everyone simmers and stews
we reach for the midnight aspirin,
by now not half-expecting it
to take away the ache of generations

we wake up to the waning of the darkness
in the cold and stiffened daycreep of first light
and not one of us can help but be reminded
of just who and where we aren't

You Are Here

in a place like this
you feel the cold before it's cold –
you turn to drink to keep you warm

in a place like this
you never listen to your heart –
there's not much left to think about
that anyone still cares to think about

in a place like this
we've traded our forests for orchards
our rivers for canals
we've converted our prairies to cropland
and replaced our thundering herds
with hamburger on the hoof

in a place like this
you lead a tertiary existence:
eight hours of every twenty-four
you work, another eight you sleep,
and the eight you have left over
are the ones you try to live in

in a place like this
the carrot jiggles enticingly –
the stick is getting longer by the day

and in the toll of distant timeworn bells
that mark each seventh dawn
what used to be our opiate
seems more like our placebo

Graveyard Shift

I get off on getting off –
on getting off before the dawn:

the oranging in the east,
the lightening eoscene
of powder blue expanses –
not-yet-ugly cityscapes,
the burning in the eyes
of nightlong labor

I end my day before
the day begins again

I turn the key
and stab the gas,
get up on top
of wound-out gears
and I head west
against the traffic
on its caffeine-zombied
wide-eyed way to work

Inhabitance

these eyes have seen the scenery
alive with living things
and lingered long enough
to watch them die

and though they fill my lonely life
with memories and regret
well, this is where I live
when I'm alive

those songs sing so much deeper now –
the rhyme rings truer still,
enough to make you shake
your head and cry

the air is rife with dissonance,
the music of discord –
and this is where I live
when I'm alive

the nights seem so much shorter than
they did when I was young –
I think I'm just beginning
to see why:

there's so much more to live down
than there was to live up to,
so this is where I live
when I'm alive

they say you can't go home again –
they're pretty sure of that,
like no one's ever lived
beyond good bye

I may've been away for some
unnumbered sum of days,
but this is where I lived
when I's alive

Vertebrates Of The United States

It was the 1957 edition, a John Glenn High School
library copy I had become completely immersed in
during those sophomoric days of Westland, MI.

Yep, there it was on that sunny afternoon
in late January 1972, sailing smartly through the
wintry air, pages fluttering helplessly as it passed
from one big burly eleventh-grader to the next.

The rest of my books had already come to rest in
the snow as the morbidly curious crowd began to
gather in the field. As often as I pondered the point,
I never came to figure out why it always took three
bigger guys to beat the crap out of the skinniest kid
in the school – and why no one ever intervened to
lend a hand.

"Ha-ha, check this shit out – hey, Poindexter, what's
a vertebrate?"

No sense in trying to answer, or even in trying too
vigorously to intercept the hapless volume. It's not
like they had any intention of dropping it until
they'd sufficiently amused themselves. The book
(and I) would fare better if I just acted as dorklessly
as possible, kept my mouth shut, and endured a little
shoving around. The sooner I was thoroughly
humiliated, the sooner it would all be over.

The inevitable combination of kick in the shin and shove in the back sent me sprawling facedown in the stinging white powder, much to the delight of the not-so-innocent bystanders. Might as well just stay down. It looked as though the book was miraculously still intact and lying a few yards away, and that was the important thing.

A couple more swift kicks and a good solid smush-down of my head into the frozen sod and they were done. The onlookers reluctantly retreated, casting a few last smirking comments over their shoulders...

Well, that was adolescence. A few long-forgotten superficial scrapes. An equal number of deeply-festering inner wounds.

Ah, but we get over all that kid-stuff, right?

Right?

Nebulosity

I wake up in the evening
and I listen
to the whispers of the wind
as translated by the trees
and, though I don't speak
the language,
I can't help but understand

in the glow
of the crystalline distance
and the magnified miles of air –
languishing in loneliness,
so many things come clear

I have watched the deep
impatient surging of the clouds
so grey in their migration
as they march across the sky
silvered as they pass
before the moon

I have hovered in the hope and dread
of brave tomorrow's dark demise
settling out as dew upon the lawn

and I have felt you
in ways I can't seem to
whenever we're both in one place

Brontitude

southeastern Michigan in late summer

the distant flash of cracking sky
reverberates throughout
this greenly-wooded
rolling-meadowed land

you smell the coming of the rain
and hear the graveled wash
of rolling rubber passing by

you taste the twist of sorrow
in your own recumbent tongue

and through the toss and turn and tumble
of the leaves upon the wind
your eyes caress the ashen mantle
as it swiftly glides away

but all you feel now
is a deep and longing
thirstiness of heart
unquenchable as the history
that's been stealing past your home
in all the many years you've been away

IDK

IDK with every LOL
and OMG and YOLO,
every hashtag,
LMAO, smiley face,
thumbs-up emoji
and that cute little brown
pile of dookie (WTF??)

IDK with every tweet
and my inability
to do more with the
language than reduce
it to a series of mindless
sub-hieroglyphics

IDK and disappear
into the grammarless
illiteracy of spellbound
acronymity gone wordless

To Have Had *(and now)*

poring over volumes
I could read so easily
before my eyes
began to fail me
among the library's
shelves upon shelves
where I once climbed
to the top of the book stacks
to get a good look at the world

gazing across the landscape
at the distances once traversed
(and others I know I *could* have)
when I was so much more ambulatory

standing helpless
in the dimly-lit garage
picking up the tools
I've lost my grip on
after all these years of labor

sitting at my laptop
trying to remember
what it was that I was
just distractedly writing about
and hoping against hope
that my memory is still more robust
than the hard-drive after hard-drive
that have crashed before my eyes

I fling my arms across the workspace
sweeping Siri, Alexa, and Wikipedia
to the hardwood floors of my still-undemented prison
and lamenting loudly the lack of an actual Hell
that both Bill Gates and Steve Jobs
could be condemned to eternally rot in

From Here To Uncertainty

the slowly-
sky-crossed sun
seems to hint at
an unhurried
and eternal
turn of Earth

where we not only
have forever
but we can make
the same mistake
of not making anything
of this day
or the next day
or the next

whereas the wind
in all its swirling restlessness
whispers its reminders
that tomorrow
is a finite proposition

as uncertain
as today was
yesterday

Some Assumptions

you thought you'd just keep walking,
your resilient sense of sole
would persist and propel you
over any and all terrain

no destination distant enough
to be unreachable –
the march of time
would never overstep
your thirsty boots

but now, your legs gone leaden,
feel those sprawling green
expanses rolling back
upon the curling
of your map

you thought you'd just keep seeing,
that your eyes would always
penetrate the smoke and mirrors
of flimsy advertising,
the dark headlightless highway,
and the fine print
tucked so neatly underfont

but now, the blinding incandescence
of an unsated dynamo
usurps your weary vision
and swaps it for this cropped and
photoshop-enhanced illusion
of some fairy-taled future:
one hallucination under
Bill/Melinda God

you thought you'd just keep working,
that there'd never come a day
when you'd outlive your
life-sustaining usefulness

there would always be a reason
to rise up to face the morning
with your block-and-tackle back,
your flexion-steeled joints,
and the tools of a lifetime
still so firmly in your grasp

but now your plans have stiffened,
your resolve has rusted-fast,
the grease has gone to gravy
in your gears

you thought you'd just keep thinking,
never numbed by the negligence
of knowing nor unnerved
by the know-it-alls who
browbeat those who don't

skeptical of every easy answer,
unafraid of leaving questions
still unplugged for as long
as it may take to
fully quench them

but now your long-encumbered
reasoning unravels at the seams,
plagued as much by doubt
as mere dementia

you thought you'd just keep feeling
everything there was to feel,
all the pain and anger,
sorrow, apprehension
of what goes on within you
and without you

forever grappling with the phony joy
and sin-forgiven guiltlessness,
the suffering all around
of everyone who's worse off
yet than you

and now you know the only thing
you were always right about,
in the failing of your arms and legs,
your eyes and ears, your brain, your back,
your bladder and your bowels

one part of you remains
to take its beatings
and its bleeding
to the end

Stolen Moments Of Gladness #3: *words and music*

OK, you win. I have to admit there is some scant
amount of happiness to be had. Right here amongst
the rubble of this sprawling anthropocentric
landscape; this trampled and castrated biosphere;
this digitally dumbed-down, over-automated,
selfie-posing cardboard cutout of humanity we
bestow Oscar after Emmy after Grammy after
Pulitzer upon.

But, fuck all that, and tell me —
is there anything in this world to compare to:

The way Alex Chilton growls *Give me a ticket for
an aeroplane...* just as you're sailing down that
work-bound onramp and cursing your miserable,
back-breaking blue-collar life?

The way The Drifters can take you *Up on the roof*
in those elusive rejuvenate hours that seem to be all
you'll ever be able to claim as your own in the
wake of another day's merciless beatings?

The way you can't help but join in with Bob as he
belts out that sneering, *How does it feeeel...?*

The way your eyes roll over until you can see the
back of your own skull when Bruce sings out
*For the ones who had a notion, a notion deep
inside, that it ain't no sin to be glad you're alive?*

The guitar solo that intervenes to shatter the
sleepless desperation of Chicago's "25 or 6 to 4"?

The way David Byrne reminds you *This ain't no party; this ain't no disco; this ain't no foolin' around!?*

The swirling transcendence of The Pretenders' "Back On The Chain Gang"?

The mournful exhilaration and driving drone of 1980s-vintage R.E.M.?

Lee Dorsey's plaintive *Lord, I'm so tired; how long can this go on?*, Sam Cooke's parched *Give me water; I'm thirsty; my work is so hard* or Otis Redding's beleaguered *I can't do what ten people tell me to do?*

The oozing sarcasm of The Kinks' "Dedicated Follower Of Fashion", "A Well-Respected Man" or "Sunny Afternoon"?

The screaming disquietude of the guitars and John's voice as "Revolution" bursts forth from whatever speakers it just laid waste to?

The distilled disillusionment of Simon and Garfunkel and their long, world-weary migration from swearing that *I have no need of friendship; friendship causes pain; it's laughter and it's loving I disdain* to declaring *There were times when I was so lonesome I took some comfort there...?*

Screw the sex and drugs, rock & roll is at its best when it is living up to its real job as the poetry of the people – the thinking, feeling, working, breathing people.

Making America Grate Again

the promise of the loud and proud
sounds grate upon my ears
echoing the thundered heavy mettle
of the lost-and-founding fathers
and the mothers of infection
to the fattened franchised fanfare
of at least a hundred thousand
trumpeteers:

> "O Plangaea – O mighty Plangaea,
> so flat and front and center
> and as obvious as ever
> to anyone who's earned his leather,
> who doesn't need a climatologist
> to know which way the wind blows
> or some environmental retard
> to tell him how to play
> the fish and game
>
> I was born here – lucky me,
> in the red and whitened blue
> of collars raised a-loan
> upon a minimum of wage,
> and what you wanna work for
> when you can just win the lotto
> or shift your way into American idle??"

By God, how grate thy science!
By Country, how grate thou art:
Erica, God Bless 'Em!
Erica, God Bless 'Em!
Erica, God Bless 'Em!
and on and on *e pluribus infinitum*★...

★don't forget to be fruitful and multiply!

Some Concessions

take my back if you must –
it's already halfway gone
now anyway

pry loose my grip
on these wrenches,
hammers, shovels,
these binoculars and pens,
as soon as I lose my effectiveness
in wielding them to some end

slow my run to a walk,
then to a stagger
and a crawl –
I figure I've gone just
about as far as I could've

close my eyes to the blinding
white light of mid-day and spare me
having to watch it all further decay

but let me pass undemented
into that all-encompassing darkness
that awaits every life form
at the end of its living

and please lend no quiescence
to the leaping and the plunging
of my heart
in anger at what is,
sorrow for what was,
and fear of what or what's not
yet to come

Under The Melanosphere

across the wide black ocean
I make eyefall
as wave on wave
of distant recollection
laps the jagged unseen shore
so many feet beneath my feet

where seasung birds sail headlong
through luminous wakefulness
all along this fleeting maritime of night

and I remember my life lessens
with every lunar phase
as I retread the sleepless gleaming
of hours that were never far from dark

Before The Fall

though far more subtle here
than where I used to live,
with some years practice
you'll discern it just the same

that rare, impatient character
the autumn air assumes,
each afternoon gone sooner –
deeper gold,
as if ushered into evening
by the wind

and, though we have less
than the rest of September
to spirit the summer away,
there is a far and widened
calmness in the sky

as all the landscape grows October,
so stunningly-seasoned and sober,
you won't find a better time
for taking stock of all the colors
you once were and have become

Awaiting October Again

it takes so long to learn to live –
it takes even longer to learn how to die

and all these "little crises"
you belittle me for belaboring
seem to me to coalesce into one
pervasive and ponderous whole

it's easy to say, "don't dwell on it"
but every time I look around,
somebody else is gone

can you honestly not see
that there are no little deaths –
every one of them is the same size,
no matter who it happens to:
each one is big enough
to exactly negate a life

and every life that goes away –
well, have you ever actually seen
any one of them return???

look, I know long-longed-for October
is on its way, but the burning question is:

could this finally be the year
when that makes no difference?

Who Would Want To Be The Last?

in some deep
and numberless hour
of some vague
and nameless night
so very near the end
of another anonymous bio
about to be tossed to the lost
and found

the barest of threads
dangle helplessly –
the fabric of a lifetime
come unraveled
by the passage
of acquaintances
and landmarks

flesh and blood
have finally come
to equilibrium
as some unknown soul
goes missing in the darkness

and in another lonely corner
of the same black monochrome
another someone wakes

to realize his life
has come to naught
though no ending's
yet in sight –
this same nothingness
will drag on
for some years now

Until I Come To Rest

some of the time left I labor
happily hammering away
at this huge amorphous mound
of long-unfinished work

and I wonder how much any of this
matters to anyone but me

some of the time left I wander
from highway to hilltop
and shadows to shore
just trying to take it all in

and I wonder how so much
of it still escapes me

some of the time left I slumber
at least until my conscience intervenes
and drags me from my dreamlessness
back up to day's unrest

and I wonder why
I even sleep at all

some of the time left I sit here
on the edge of the night and my bed
with the same old silence seeping through
the numbness of all this new improved noise

and I wonder where it is
they've all gotten off to

Early Autumn Morning In The Desert
With Clouds And Terrain

I'm walking on the rocks
and sand across a bone-strewn land,
held live by will-be winter bush
that's going nowhere soon

I'm talking nonsense to myself
and everyone I ever knew:

thanking all my elders,
most of whom are gone by now,
for all the sustenance
that's driven me this far

reassuring those
who'll fight these fights
long after I subside
by singing songs out loud,
from Tom Petty to Fats Domino
and almost everyone between

I have a home not far from here
where I'll find water too

and until then I'll see how far I go
on a breakfast burrito *sin carne*
and a shot of dear Melinda's triple-X

November No More

it's October's after-equinox –
the ambered autumn air,
the coppery senescence
of the sun set sail for solstice
on the arc of Earth's illusion

it's the scarlet, sulfur
flaming of the forests
in farewell

it's the way you watch
so flightlessly
the wave on wave
of outward-bound
as they join the distant sky
and disappear

it's that hallowed when of whens
each year must funnel through
on its lonely way to winter
once again

it's all these things embodied
in the night of the living,
day of the dead –
anticipation come confused
with recollection
of life after life,
afterlife presupposed

and each new wind
that comes astir
of the now-denuded trees
blows a little colder
than the last

in the ache of all these seasons,
you find you need no calendar
to know it's November no more

Eleventh Month, Eleventh Hour

so very late in the day
in a season weekly-creeping
to completion,
somehow the disillusioned
soldier on

to the decrepitude of body
and disgruntlement of soul,
if not yet the dreaded bliss
of the dementia of mind

but all their reasoning, ideas,
and their memory and plans –
these will not go gentle
into any known "good night"

they will remember, miss, and mourn
every soul that touched their own

they will continue to envision
the fruition come of labored
generations fore and aft

they will persevere in cursive
of all deities and demons
and both heavenly
and hellish guarantees

and they will piss into
the roaring maw of death

Untold Winter Stories

I suppose I could've told you once

how the yule tide ebbs
and the twinkle of winter wears off

how deep, dark December's extended Janu-wariness
tears mercilessly at last year's stubborn final pages

how bleakened February's streetscapes gleam
with semi-thawed/refrozen slush —
what once was snow, gone ashen
in a dozen nameless shades of grey,
interspersed with gravel, broken asphalt,
grease and oil, and the sooty Motown fall-out
of this stark blue-collar capital of the world

I suppose I could've told you once again

how the ice clings to the unrelenting March
that tramples long-overdue greenspans
and throttles any thought
of some far-distant re-chlorescence,
leaving all the land so undoggedly dead-brown
from here to the hazy horizon

yes, I suppose I could've told you once and for all

but all those lonely onces, in the end, don't sum
to much as bravely feeble last bonflickerings
predictably succumb to the fierce bone-rattling
onslaught of the winds

Unencumbered By Slumber

How can you even think
about sleeping
when the night's all over you?

When darkness sets itself
upon the world
to hold the light in check?

I am awake.

I am alive.

My heart aches
for all that's been
and yearns
for what still could be
and settles in
to find the stillness
of the moment.

My head is spinning,
yet undizzied
in the quickened clarity
and the dreamless tangibility
that belongs to these rare
and shining afterhours.

I can taste the sky
and I can hear the clouds.

I can feel the shimmering
of midnight on the waters
and I can sense the hard
and warm terrain.

I can smell the fear
of living slowly
melting away.

I can see most everything
the noise of day conceals.

And I curse myself
for ever having
learned to go to sleep

You're Still The You Of Your Youth

even as the scores of seasons
pile up outside
while lofty dreams
still tower over
actual accomplishments

even as both girth and stature
radiate away
from younger heartwood

even though the losses
always seem to outnumber the wins
when you swore
from the beginning
you weren't playing

even though decay
has come to far-outstrip
all growth
and the dying is rapidly
overtaking the living

even as the yearning restlessness
gives way to not-so-quiet resignation

it's still you
so long, deep down there
at the bottom of your birthdays –
that youngest you has outlived
every later iteration
and it'll be that very last
glint in your eye
when everything else
you've been
may somehow
have fallen away

Gravicardia

when your heart
has grown so heavy
with the burden
of the world
(all the lives it's lost
and still keeps
losing by the day)
that you don't know
how much longer
you can hold it
front and center
in your breast

before too long
it will be sinking
deeper, deeper
into you

pulling lungs
and breath alike
down alongside it
as you whisper
"let me go"

"just let me go"

Serving This Unpunctuated Sentence

in a dark and deafened room I sit
watching all I was and would have been
oozing oh so slowly out of me

and trickling down the table legs
to bleed into the rug
not four feet shy of bookshelves
cast in shades of afternoon

a wasted mass of protoplasm
sticking to the chair

Someplace(s) in Detroit:

A. Birthplace: Detroit Osteopathic Hospital (abandoned since 2012)
B. Residence 1 (1956-1962): 20254 San Juan, Detroit
C. Residence 2 (1963-1979): 333 S Byfield, Westland
D. John Glenn High
E. Henry Ford Community College
F. Wayne Assembly Plant (Ford Motor Co)

1. Belle Isle (just north of the US/Canada border in the Detroit River)
2. Detroit to Windsor tunnel
3. Ambassador Bridge
4. Detroit Zoo

Subfossil Snapshot

mind your arms and legs
and whether you're prone
supine or fetal
and the angle
of your head
upon the ground

this is how
they'll find you
if they find you
some ten thousand
years from now
in the thaw
forsaken valley
where you finally
found your rest

Appendix A: Motown to Mojave *(and back again, over and over and over)* — *this volume's poems in chronologic order:*

2016

2017

2018

[1]previously published in *Altadena Poetry Review*
(Anthology 2018)
[2]previously published online at *Wisdom Quarterly*
(January 15, 2018)
[3]previously published in *Spectrum 14*
(Spectrum Publishing, March 2018)
[4]the 1300th poem in 39 years, for whatever *that's* worth

Appendix B: **Milestones And Kidney Stones –** *somehow we've passed them all:*

2018

04 Jan	Moody Blues founding member Ray Thomas died at 76.
14 Jan	Hall of Fame race car driver and builder Dan Gurney died at 86.
20 Jan	Zombies/Kinks bassist Jim Rodford died at 76.
11 Feb	Comedian Marty Allen died at 95.
21 Feb	Evangelist Billy Graham died at 99.
26 Feb	Close friend Keith Westwood lost his wife Joy (she was 57).
10 Mar	Close friend Mark Boyak died at 59.
14 Mar	Physicist Stephen Hawking died at 76.
19 Mar	The northern subspecies of square-lipped rhinoceros *(Ceratotherium simum cottoni)* effectively became extinct, which does not mean the species is gone (in fact, with a world-wide population estimated at 21,000, it is the only one of the five living rhinoceros species that is not *critically* endangered) – let's quit jerking off with the idea of GMO "northern white rhinos" and start concentrating on *Diceros bicornis*[1] (less than 5000 left), *Rhinoceros unicornis*[2] (< 3000 left), *Dicerorhinus sumatrensis*[3] (< 300 left), and *Rhinoceros sondaicus*[4] (< 50 left)!
17 Apr	41st First Lady Barbara Bush died at 92.
15 Jun	Guitarist Matt Murphy died at 88.
19 Jun	ASL-fluent, cat-loving western gorilla Koko died at 46 (BTW, both species of gorillas are critically endangered).

22 Jun	*Land Of The Giants* actress Deanna Lund died at 81.
30 Jun	Close friend Ken Gentile lost his mom Dale (she was 87).
16 Aug	Singer Aretha Franklin died at 76.
20 Aug	Motown Funk Brothers guitarist Eddie Willis died at 82, leaving only 2 of the original 13 (percussionist Jack Ashford and guitarist Jose Messina) still alive.
22 Aug	Close friend Roberta Valdemar died at 61.
25 Aug	Vietnam War POW and runner-up for 44th President John McCain died at 81.
26 Aug	Playwright Neil Simon died at 91.
06 Sep	*Deliverance* co-star Burt Reynolds died at 82.
02 Oct	Prominent Beatles engineer Geoff Emerick died at 72.
11 Nov	Douglas Rain (the voice of HAL in *2001: A Space Odyssey*) died at 90.
12 Nov	Marvel Comics writer Stan Lee (co-creator of Spiderman, The Incredible Hulk and a host of others) died at 95.
12 Nov	Legendary stock car driver David Pearson, who won more races than any NASCAR driver other than Richard Petty (105 and 200 lifetime races, respectively) died at 83.
15 Nov	Country music singer/musician Roy Clark died at 85.
30 Nov	41st President George H. W. Bush died at 94.
18 Dec	Actress Penny Marshall died at 75.

1968 (50 years ago):

01 Jan	The second edition of Ernest P. Walker's *Mammals of the World* was published.
02 Jan	The first successful heart transplant was performed by Dr. Christiaan Barnard in South Africa.
23 Jan	North Korea seized the USS Pueblo.
30 Jan	The Tet offensive was launched by North Vietnam.
16 Feb	The first 9-1-1 emergency phone call was made in Haleyville, Alabama.
16 Mar	500 unarmed civilians were slaughtered by US troops in My Lai, S.Vietnam.
22 Mar	The 1968 Cougar I have driven since 1990 rolled off the assembly line.
01 Apr	The 428 Cobra Jet engine was introduced by Ford.
03 Apr	Simon and Garfunkel's 4th of 5 albums *(Bookends)* was released.
03 Apr	The original *Planet Of The Apes* came to theaters.
04 Apr	Martin Luther King, Jr. was assassinated.
11 Apr	The Civil Rights Act of 1968 was signed.
12 May	*2001: A Space Odyssey* came to theaters (see 11 Nov 2018 above).
13 May	42 days of occupation of "Resurrection City" in Washington, D. C. began as part of the Poor People's Campaign led by Rev. Ralph Abernathy.
25 May	The Gateway Arch in St. Louis was inaugurated.
29 May	The Truth in Lending Act was signed.
01 Jun	The second edition of *Vertebrates of the United States* was published.
05 Jun	Robert Kennedy was assassinated.
15 Jun	Prince (my 1st dog) was 10 years old.

22 Jun	Pirate (my 2nd dog) was born.
28 Aug	The police riot during the Democratic National Convention that led to "The Chicago 8" grand jury trial occurred.
30 Aug	The single "Hey Jude/Revolution" was released by The Beatles.
23 Sep	*Charly* came to theaters.
29 Sep	A Ford GT-40 won the 24 hours of Le Mans (for the 3rd of 4 consecutive years) even after the factory withdrew official support and the engine size limit was reduced from 7 to 5 liters.
30 Sep	The Boeing 747 began flying.
02 Oct	Redwood National Park was established.
04 Oct	*Night Of The Living Dead* came to theaters.
10 Oct	The hometown team prevailed over the St. Louis Cardinals in 7 games to win the last "divisionless" World Series.
16 Oct	Tommie Smith, Peter Norman, and John Carlos (gold, silver, and bronze medalists for the 200 meter dash) each wore the patch of the Olympic Project for Human Rights to the podium during the 1968 Olympics medal ceremony where Smith and Carlos raised the Black Power salute.
17 Oct	*Bullitt* came to theaters.
03 Nov	At the end of the NASCAR season, Ford 427s in Torinos and Cyclones (sometimes de-stroked to 396 in^3) had won 27 of 49 races; David Pearson (see 12 Nov 2018) won the driver's championship in a Holman-Moody Ford.
22 Nov	*The Beatles* (aka "The White Album") was released.
21 Dec	Apollo 8 became the first manned spacecraft to orbit the moon, beaming back photos of "Earthrise on the moon".

1918 (100 years ago):

17 Feb	My father was born.
21 Feb	The last Carolina parakeet (*Conuropsis carolinensis*) died in the same cage of the same zoo (Cincinnati) that the last passenger pigeon (*Ectopistes migratorius*) died in on 01 Sep 1914.
19 Mar	US time zones were established and daylight saving time was approved.
02 May	General Motors acquired Chevrolet.
15 May	Airmail service began between NYC, Philadelphia, and Washington, D. C.
16 May	The Sedition Act of 1918 was signed.
11 Nov	"The war to end all wars" ended – kind of gives you that warm, fuzzy feeling of optimism, doesn't it?

[1] the African hook-lipped (aka "black") rhino
[2] the Indian rhino
[3] the Sumatran rhino
[4] the Javan rhino

(see the *IUCN Red List* for the status of any species)

Photo credit: Luz Aguilar

Since 1979, Detroit-born Joseph Nicks has divided his waking hours more-or-less equally between his "day job" and his nocturnal writing. The diurnal component has varied from manual laborer to water quality lab technician, assistant science advisor to a museum exhibits development team, technical writer, public school biology teacher, and field biologist. He holds a B.S. in terrestrial zoology and two teaching credentials (multiple subject and single subject/biology) and currently lives in a small town in the Mojave Desert.

Recent publications include *Tales From The Otherground* (2014) and *Songs From The Dirt* (2015).